Anonymous

Overland Journey of the Governor of New Zealand

Anonymous

Overland Journey of the Governor of New Zealand

ISBN/EAN: 9783337216184

Printed in Europe, USA, Canada, Australia, Japan

Cover: Foto ©Andreas Hilbeck / pixelio.de

More available books at **www.hansebooks.com**

OVERLAND JOURNEY

OF THE

GOVERNOR OF NEW ZEALAND.

———•◦❖◦•———

NOTES OF THE JOURNEY

OF

SIR GEORGE F. BOWEN, G.C.M.G.,

IN APRIL, 1872,

FROM

WELLINGTON TO AUCKLAND,

ACROSS THE CENTRE OF THE

NORTH ISLAND OF NEW ZEALAND.

WITH AN APPENDIX,

Containing Letters from Maori Chiefs to the Agent-General.

———•◦❖◦•———

LONDON:

G. STREET, 30, CORNHILL.

1872.

OVERLAND JOURNEY

OF THE

GOVERNOR OF NEW ZEALAND.

————◦◦————

GOVERNOR SIR GEORGE BOWEN had for
some time determined to travel overland across
the central and recently hostile districts of New
Zealand, for all those best qualified to judge were of
opinion that a visit from the representative of the
Queen to the Maori clans of the interior would be
productive of great public advantage to the colony.
In the first place it would powerfully help to confirm
in their loyalty the well-affected natives, and also to
bring back to their allegiance those recently in arms
against the Queen; in the second place, the fact of the
Governor having himself traversed in safety and confidence districts lately inaccessible to Europeans would
be considered in England a proof of the restored tranquillity of the country, and would thus exercise a
favourable influence in promoting immigration to New
Zealand.

The overland route between Wellington and Auckland is by Napier (the chief town of the province of
Hawke's Bay) and by the great inland lake of Taupo.

The country between Wellington and Napier has now for several years been occupied by pastoral and agricultural settlers; and the few Maoris resident among them, belonging chiefly to the clans of the Ngatiawa and Ngatikahungunu, are well affected to the Government, and live on the most friendly terms with their white neighbours.

A good carriage road has already been completed northwards from Wellington to Masterton, a distance of some 70 miles, and from Napier southwards to Porangahau, about 80 miles, and coaches carrying mails and passengers run regularly to and from those places. The gap between Masterton and Porangahau does not exceed 90 miles, and will be filled up ere long, as roads are being pushed on steadily in all the settled districts in accordance with a well-considered plan.

As the Governor had already seen much of the country between Wellington and Napier, and as there was no public object to be gained by travelling overland in this part of his journey, he proceeded by sea in the Government steamer " Luna," leaving Wellington on the 2nd April, and, after a stormy passage, reaching Napier on the evening of the 3rd.

His Excellency remained here during the 4th and 5th, visiting the public institutions in the town and the neighbouring " kaingas," or villages, of Pakowhai and Waiohiki. The large sums paid to the natives as rents by the pastoral settlers (amounting lately to £26,000 a year), as well as the produce of land sales (all divided among about 200 Maori families) have enabled the native chiefs near Napier to build good houses in the English style, and to live in English comfort. They have good carriages, horses, cattle, and well-cultivated farms. One very interesting fact is the establishment by the natives at Pakowhai of a school where the children are now going through all the usual course of an English education, and show remarkable proficiency.

While on the subject of native schools it may be observed that this branch of civilisation has been warmly taken up by the Colonial Government; an annual subsidy extending over a course of years has been voted by Parliament, and devoted strictly to the object it was intended to attain; and it is a pleasing fact that a wide-spread disposition exists among the natives to impart to their children the benefits of education. It has been found by experience that the readiest method of instilling European habits into the natives is by teaching them the English language, and enlarging their understandings by acquainting them with the nature and geography of other countries in addition to the usual routine of daily school life. In many cases the result has exceeded all anticipation, the children being excessively quick at picking up the language of the pakeha, and very apt at figures and penmanship.

Napier until lately was the outpost of colonisation towards the interior. In 1866 a sharply contested battle was fought by the colonial forces with the insurgents at Omaranui, eight miles from the town; and it is within only the last two years that the neighbourhood has been safe from hostile incursions. The

Colonial Government are rapidly pushing on a road from Napier to Taupo, the geographical and strategical centre of the island. This road is being made chiefly by native labour, and is protected by five small detachments of the colonial forces, placed in stockaded posts, connected together by the electric telegraph, at Te Haroto, Tarawera, Runanga, Opepe, and Tapuaeharuru (at the northern end of Lake Taupo). .

On April 6th the Governor left Napier for Taupo, accompanied by one A.D.C; by Mr. Locke, the Civil Commissioner of the district, and by the Master of Blantyre, who has been for some time travelling in the Australasian colonies. The coach-road has already been finished to the Mohaka river, about 30 miles from Napier, and, now that permanent tranquillity has been established, the country through which it passes will soon be occupied by settlers. The Governor and his party slept this night at the post at Te Haroto, occupied by the Colonial forces, 35 miles from Napier. It occupies a strong position, 2,200 feet above the sea, on a summit of a high hill commanding a magnificent view of the sea and of the coast, as well as of the wild mountains and forests of the Urewera country to the eastward.

On the 7th the Governor started on horseback at 7 a.m., and after a ride of 42 miles reached Opepe at 7 p.m., another post of the colonial forces, where he again slept. The party had been joined at Te Haroto by Major Scannell, commanding the district, and had stopped for breakfast and lunch respectively at the posts of Tarawera and Runanga. The carriage road has not yet been completed throughout the distance travelled this day, but there is already a good bridle track. Much of the land is rich, and the mountain and forest scenery is very beautiful, reminding the European traveller of the Italian slopes of the Alps. Contracts for the completion of the road have been taken by the Maoris of Taupo, and it will be finished in the course of the present year, when a coach will run regularly from Napier to the Lake, carrying mails and passengers to the heart of the island. A tri-weekly coach service already exists from Auckland to Cambridge, in the Waikato, a distance of about 120 miles ; and the break between Cambridge and Taupo is only some 70 miles. Of this gap a considerable portion has already been filled up by native labour, and the carriage road throughout will probably be completed in the course of a twelvemonth ; when coaches will be able to travel from Napier (and soon from Wellington also) to Auckland in about four days, stopping each night at the inns already finished, or in process of erection. A statement asserting the possibility of such a fact would have appeared incredible three years ago, when the natives of the central districts were for the most part in active or sullen hostility. On the 8th the Governor left Opepe, at a distance from which of some 10 miles, an hour's ride along a good road, lies the great lake of Taupo, 1,250 feet above the sea, and resembling in its extent (about 200 square miles of water) and in scenery, the Lake of Geneva. On his arrival at Tapuaeharuru, the native settlement at the north end of the lake, and near the point where the river

Waikato issues from it, the Governor was enthu-
siastically received by the well-known chief Poihipi
Tukairangi, one of the signers of the Treaty of Waitangi,
and by his people, with whom was held a korero, or
conference. The following is a brief summary of the
speeches delivered:—

POIHIPI TUKAIRANGI said: Welcome, O Governor,
to Taupo! We have been long desiring to see you.
For many years past we have been in great trouble.
We were nearly destroyed; still a few of us have
always remained firm to the Queen, and like the
Horomatangi (sea god) that dwelt of yore in Lake
Taupo, and in former days swallowed the evil monsters
of the deep, we have now destroyed our enemies; but
our joy at welcoming you to Taupo recompenses us for
the past troubles. Taupo is yours, the lake, and all
the lands around, and all the people. Take them all.
You come as the sign of peace. Welcome! for you
are our father. We desire to commemorate your
arrival amongst us by naming some place after you.
We should like that the town to be founded here
should be called after you. We feel now as if new
life were given us, when we see the Governor in our
midst. We know that we are not forgotten. The
people now here represent the feeling of the whole
tribe. Welcome! Welcome! (Then followed a song
of welcome, in the chorus of which all joined).

REWETI TE KUME said: Welcome, O Governor,
to Taupo! Come and instruct us in all the laws,
thoughts, and works of the Europeans. Taupo is
yours, the lake, the people, and the land: yours to

carry out the works of the Europeans—to make roads
and other works, and to have schools to teach our
children English. There have been Hauhaus amongst
us, but all are yours now. Whatever your plans may
be respecting this country, we are waiting to carry
them out. (Another song of welcome followed.)

PAORA RAUHIHI said: Welcome, O Governor, to
Taupo! We have long been wishing to see you. We
have often heard of you by name, but we thought we
should never see your face here. Welcome to Taupo.
(Another song of welcome). I never saw a Governor
before. We are but a remnant of what we once were.
Welcome.

His EXCELLENCY then spoke nearly as follows: O
my friends, chiefs and people of Ngatituwharetoa,
salutations to you all. You in particular, O Poihipi
Tukairangi, I salute, for you have ever been loyal to
the Queen and a firm friend to the English, nor is this
the first time that you have welcomed me. When I
first arrived in New Zealand, four years ago, you
wrote me a letter of welcome. That letter, together
with other letters from loyal Maori chiefs, was sent to
the Queen's Ministers in England, and it was afterwards printed with other documents respecting this
country, for the information of the great parliament of
the Empire at London ; so the name of Poihipi
Tukairangi is now spread far and wide. The English
naval officer, Lieutenant Meade, who came to Taupo
in 1865, and was so hospitably entertained by you here,
has also written a book in which your loyalty, and the
beauty of your lakes and mountains are celebrated.

In the wars and troubles of the last few years, Poihipi has stood firm to the Queen, even as the rocky isle of Motu Taiko, now before us, stands firm as ever amid the winds and waves of the great lake. When evil times came on, and the sky was dark and lowering, the friends of law and order took refuge with him, even as canoes caught by a storm take refuge under the lee of Motu Taiko. Now the storm is passing away; the sun shines forth again; and the tribes lately disaffected are returning to their allegiance, and are following his good example. In a word, the influence of Poihipi (as he himself said just now) has driven away the demons of war and murder which were devastating this fair land, even as the sea-god Horomatangi, celebrated in the old Maori legends, destroyed the taniwhas (sea monsters) which once infested the shores of the lake of Taupo. And now, my friends, I rejoice that you are industrious in peace as you have been brave in war. You were the first to join the Government in making the roads through your district, those roads which confer such great benefits on all alike—on the Maoris and on the pakehas. I trust you will also join the Government in founding schools, as your countrymen have already done at Pakowhai, Maketu, and elsewhere. Thus your children will grow up in good nurture, well-educated, and able to cultivate the arts of peace, and live in friendship and harmony with the English. Then the two nations, the white skin and the brown, which inhabit this island, will grow up into one people, with common laws and institutions. O, my friends, I pray that God, the Giver of all good, may pour his choicest gifts upon you all. (The Governor's speech was greeted with loud cheers by the natives.)

The name Tapuaeharuru signifies "resounding footsteps," and has reference to the hollow sound of the earth from the volcanic action which extends throughout the zone, reaching from the great burning mountain of Tongariro south of Taupo to Whakari, or White Island, also an active volcano, in the Bay of Plenty, a distance of 120 miles. Hot springs and geysers abound throughout this region, one of the most interesting and wonderful in the whole world. Good descriptions of it will be found in Hochstetter's "New Zealand," and in "A Ride through New Zealand," by Lieutenant the Hon. H. Meade, R.N. Hitherto, these grand natural phenomena have remained almost unknown; but now that tranquillity has been established, and that access to them will soon be rendered safe and easy by the completion of the roads, good inns will doubtless be erected, and New Zealand will become for the Australasian group of colonies what Switzerland and the German Baths are for Europe. The valuable medicinal qualities of these hot lakes and springs are well-known to the Maoris, who resort to them from all parts of the island for the cure of various diseases.

At the "koreros" which the Governor held with the natives in the interior, the chief requests were : first, for Queen's flags, *i.e.*, union jacks, to be hoisted at their pas, instead of the old Hauhau or rebel flags, which have been everywhere destroyed by themselves ;

secondly, that the Colonial Government should employ them in making roads through their own territories. It may here be mentioned that hundreds of Maoris lately in rebellion are now so employed. In short, the policy pursued for the pacification of the Highlands of New Zealand is (as Sir G. Bowen has often pointed out in his published despatches), the same with that adopted in the last century for the pacification of the Highlands of Scotland. The true weapons of conquest have been in both cases the spade and the pickaxe. The third request of the natives everywhere was that the Government should assist them in founding and endowing schools, where their children might learn the language and arts of the English. As has been above observed, liberal provision has been made by the Colonial Parliament for this vital object.

The Taupo natives preferred an especial request to the Governor that a European town should be founded on the shores of the Great Lake, and named "Bowen," and that a steamer should be placed on the lake. The Government will carry out all the above-mentioned requests, which are themselves proofs of the great change which has lately taken place in the sentiments of the Maoris.

On the 9th the Governor started in a whale-boat, manned by men of the Armed Constabulary, for Tokano, the chief native settlement at the south end of the lake. The distance by water is about 26 miles, and by land, along the Eastern shore, about 36 miles. The morning was clear and bright, and the great volcano of Tongariro (6,200 feet high) with smoke and steam ascending from its crater, and the lofty ridge of Ruapehu (9,200 feet above the sea), covered with perpetual snow, presented glorious features in the panorama of the mountains surrounding the lake. About noon a strong contrary gale set in, so the Governor landed at Motutere, on the eastern shore, whither horses had been sent in anticipation of one of these sudden storms, and rode the rest of the way to Tokano, a distance of about 16 miles; the boat did not reach that place till the following morning. The Governor was again received with great respect and regard by Hare Tauteka, Herekiekie, and the other chiefs and people of the clan of the Ngatituwharetoas, to whom belong Taupo and its neighbourhood. The party were lodged in Maori whares, and food was liberally provided in the absence of the supplies shipped on board the whaleboat.

Subjoined is the substance of the speeches at the korero :—

HARE TAUTEKA : Welcome, O Governor, to Taupo! It is with great joy we welcome you. We look upon you as our father, the father of the Maori people. Our number is now but few, but we welcome you with none the less sincerity. You have often shown your love to us during the past few years. We have often been told that the Governor would always be our friend, and we have found it so with you. We are rejoiced to welcome you after the troubles we have gone through, and we look to you to keep us from further trouble. (A song of welcome followed.) It gives us much pleasure, it rejoices us to have this opportunity

of welcoming you here, so that we may speak to you
as a father who takes care of us and gives us counsel
and instruction. Taupo is yours; Tongariro is yours;
they are in your hands. The Ngatituwharetoa, living
on the west shore of the lake, have come in to you.
They will require constant attention; it is only thus
you will keep those people right. Do not neglect
them. Do not neglect Taupo. Raise us up. The
country is yours; open it up. Governor Grey told us
to take care that Taupo was properly managed. He
said, " Keep Taupo together." We are now waiting
to hear what this Governor will say.

KINGI HEREKIEKIE: Welcome, O Governor, to
Taupo. Be steadfast to lead us right. Matuahu has
not long surrendered to you. We require constant
guidance, for we have but just commenced to be
wholly in the hands of the Government. Be careful
about buying land at Taupo, so that all may hear
whose land is bought, so that all may get their fair
share of the price given. Welcome, O Governor.

TOPIA TUROA: Welcome, O Governor. I belong
to Taupo as well as to Whanganui. Men and land
have been the cause of my troubles—Tawhiao and the
boundaries of our land. I was a stray sheep that
went astray, and more joy was shown at my return
than for the ninety-and-nine that had remained in the
fold. I look upon Taupo with a jealous eye; I
observe all that has been done up to the present time,
and it is all good. All that has been done here has
tended to raise the people; all has been done for the
good of the people.

WAAKA TAMAIRA : Welcome, O Governor, to Taupo. Come and visit Hare Tauteka and Te Heuheu. Welcome. Taupo and Tongariro are yours. Welcome, O friend of the people and of the country ; the friend of the people of Taupo.

HATARAKA TE WHETU : Welcome, O Governor, to Taupo and Tongariro. You have come a long and toilsome journey to visit us. Welcome to the sea of Taupo. Go and visit your home and other places, but hasten back and visit us again at Taupo

APERAHAMA TE WHETU : Welcome, O my father. We have only heard of you before; now we see you with our eyes. Look around at the land and at the lake ; they are yours. Open up the country ; assist us to make roads ; look around and see if you can improve our condition ; see what you can do to open up the country. We look to you to give us proper counsel.

KEREI TE TAKOURU : Welcome, O Governor. You will here see the result of what has been done of late. Matuahu and the others are now with us. Matuahu would have been here if we had known the exact day you were coming. We all see the benefit of this way of treating the people. You have allowed all the people of the west shore of the lake to come in. They are now firmly yours. We hope your thoughts are still for the same way of acting; if so, all are yours. We thank you for sending assistance to us when troubles came over Taupo; we will not forget your sending help when we needed it. We are all now true to the Government.

His EXCELLENCY Sir G. BOWEN then addressed the
meeting mainly as follows: O, my friends, Hare
Tauteka, Herekiekie, and all of you who have remained staunch during the late troubles, salutations to
you all! I know that you have gone through great
trials, and have shown all the gallantry of your
ancestors in war. I, as the Governor and representative of the Queen, thank you, and have now come to
visit you at your own homes. The desire of the
Queen is that her Maori and pakeha children should
grow together into one people. The Queen also is
glad that the Maoris who were lately opposed to each
other are now friends, and that all are living in peace
and harmony with the Government and the colonists.
I rejoice also to salute Topia Turoa, the stray sheep
who has returned to the fold, and who lately fought so
bravely for the Queen. I rejoice that the Ngatituwharetoa tribe is now again united, through Te
Heuheu, Matuahu, and others having submitted to the
Government. Thus all the Maoris who dwell round
the great lake of Taupo now understand the blessings
of peace, law, and order. You are already beginning
to reap the advantages of peace by selling the produce
of your labour, and thus procuring the clothes and the
other comforts of the Europeans. To carry these
benefits still further it will be well to make roads, like
your countrymen elsewhere, and as you propose to do
yourselves. The Government will assist you with
money and tools; but, mark well my words, the roads
are a benefit to the Maori as well as to the pakeha,
and the Government will not press the making of roads

through the native districts if the inhabitants of those districts object. The laws protect the land and other rights of the Maori and of the pakehas alike. No man need lease or sell his land unless he wishes it himself; the ownership (mana) of the land remains, as it has always remained, with the Maoris themselves. And now, my friends, I thank you for the hearty welcome which you have given me, and for your loyal speeches. Hare Tauteka has said that Governor Grey told him "to keep Taupo together." This is correct. I say to you the same. Keep Taupo and the Ngatitu-wharetoa in peace and harmony with the Government and with the other Maori tribes. What Te Herekiekie said on this point was very good. Before selling any land, let the titles be well ascertained, so that no disputes may arise afterwards. Do as the pakehas do. When disputes arise among you about land or any other matter, resort to the Courts, and not to fighting. There was a time, while your ancestors were living at Hawaiki, when the ancestors of the English lived much as the Maoris now live; but wise and able men arose, and taught their countrymen the arts of peace, to make roads and railways, to build ships and to found schools. You can learn all these arts from the English among you. I recommend you, therefore, to co-operate with the Government in found-ing schools for your children so that they may be taught the language and the learning of English. In this, as in all other matters, you can always apply with confidence for the aid of the Government. And now, my friends, farewell, and may all happiness attend

c

you. Be sober and industrious, and all will be well with you.

After bathing in one of the hot-springs which abound in and near Tokano, and in which the cooking of the people is carried on, the party started on the 10th for Rotoaira, the beautiful lake at the foot of Tongariro, about ten miles south of Taupo. Nothing can be more romantic than the scenery of this part of the island. From under Ruapehu and Tongariro stretch away, east, west and south, rich and well-watered valleys lying between mountain ridges, covered with the luxuriant and semi-tropical foliage of the New Zealand forests. There is no sign of human habitation in this magnificent country, but the native chiefs are already in treaty to lease large portions of it to some of the great run-holders of the South Island; and, before many years have elapsed, it will probably be covered, like the plains of Australia, with vast herds of cattle and flocks of sheep. In 1869 and 1870 there was much fighting near Tokano and Rotoaira between the colonial forces and the loyal clans on one side, and, on the other, the rebels under Te Kooti. In the afternoon the Governor rode back to Tokano, where he was again the guest of the Maori chiefs, with whom he had another korero.

On the 11th the Governor started at 9 a.m. by the boat on his return to the north end of the Lake. A small river leads from the Lake to Tokano through the alluvial plain surrounding the village, on which the natives grow a large quantity of wheat, maize, potatoes, &c. This creek must not be confounded with the Waikato river, which, rising near the foot of Ruapehu, not far from the sources of the Whanganui river (which flows to the south), enters the Taupo Lake at its southern extremity and issues from it again at Tapuaeharuru on the northern shore: from this, after a course of nearly two hundred miles, it falls into the sea on the western coast of the North Island. After entering the Lake from the Tokano creek, the Governor passed Te Rapa, the kainga of Te Heuheu, whose father, a great chief of the olden time, was, with sixty of his clansmen, overwhelmed in 1847 by an avalanche of boiling mud from the hot springs on the mountain above. His son, the present chief, joined the rebellion in 1869, but has now returned to his allegiance. A little further to the west is the mission-station of Pukawa, formerly the residence of the Rev. T. S. Grace, who was obliged to fly during the rebellion. The wind being contrary, the Governor again landed near Motutere, and rode thence in three hours to Tapuaeharuru, where there is already a small inn near the post of the colonial forces, and the pa of the loyal chief Poihipi.

On the morning of the 12th the Governor held another korero with the natives, of which the following is a summary:—

POIHIPI TUKAIRANGI: This is a welcome and a farewell to you, O Governor. This is an occasion on which all should speak out their minds, and I call on all to speak out and hide nothing from the Governor. Let the Governor go away with a full knowledge of our thoughts and our wants. Salutations to you,

O Governor, who have come to cheer us after all our troubles. I have desired to see Europeans settled at Taupo ever since I first saw them in the Bay of Islands when I signed the Treaty of Waitangi; but five Governors have come and gone, and it is only now that my hopes are being realised. We look upon this as a great blessing. Welcome, O Governor, to Taupo, and return in peace to your home.

Rawiri Kahia : Welcome, O Governor, to Taupo. Come and see for yourself the thoughts of your people, and judge of them for yourself. We are all very much rejoiced at your coming among us. I shall ever remain steadfast. We will be the same behind your back as before your face. Go home in peace. Fear not for our loyalty.

Perenaha Tamahiki (Ngatiraukawa): Welcome, O father and Governor. Here are Ngatituwharetoa and Ngatiraukawa. We are now for the Government. The tribes from all parts came and troubled and tempted us, and many left for a time, but very few remained with the Government through the troubles that have passed, but those few have gained the victory; the many are now returning. We will ever remain loyal.

Manihera : Welcome, O Governor, come to Taupo. Come and visit the people in the interior of the island : they are now all with you.

Hori Tauri : Welcome, O Governor, come and see Ngatituwharetoa and Ngatiraukawa. Come to Taupo. It cheers us up to see you at Taupo.

Hami : Come, O Governor, to Taupo and Tongariro.

Come and see Tongariro mountain, Taupo Lake, and Ngatituwharetoa tribe. Heuheu in former times was our chief, but he has long been dead. We look now to you as our chief and Governor. All those chiefs of former days that you may have heard of are dead. Poihipi and Hare Tauteka are now our elder chiefs, but you are our chief and father; you now possess all the mana.

RUTENE (Ngatiraukawa): Come, O Governor, and see your people living inland—Ngatituwharetoa and Ngatiraukawa. We now all come to Taupo as a centre, and so learn what to do, and we are now come to Taupo to meet you, and to hear from you what we should do.

TUKUREHU MAMAO: Come, O Governor. (Song of welcome.) Come, O father, for you are our guide. Come to Taupo. This tribe are now all with you.

PAURINI KARAMU: Come to Taupo. We are but few. During the past years nearly all left you: now all have returned to you. Taupo and Tongariro are yours.

POIHIPI HOROMATANGI: The Ngatituwharetoa chiefs will take care of their people, and see that no mischief arises within their boundaries. The boundaries of Taupo district are these—commencing at Horohoro; thence to Arawhena (near Titiraupenga), Maraeroa Tuhua, round by the back of the mountains to Ruapehu, on to Ruahine and Titiokura; thence to Herewiwi, and back to Horohoro. Let chiefs of other tribes be responsible for the good conduct of their own people; they must not interfere with us.

His Excellency Sir G. F. Bowen then spoke to the following effect:—O, my friends, chiefs and people of the Ngatituwharetoa, I have already addressed you in the pa of that loyal subject of the Queen, and firm friend of the pakeha, Poihipi Tukairangi. He deserves the title of Horomatangi, because he has been an enemy to all crime and evil in this district, even as, in the legend, the Horomatangi destroyed the cruel monsters (taniwhas) of the lake of Taupo. Poihipi is one of the few survivors of the chiefs who signed the Treaty of Waitangi, when the sovereignty of these islands was ceded to the Queen, who on her part engaged to protect the lands, the fisheries, and all the other rights of the Maoris. This treaty remains inviolate. The law protects the property of the Maoris as it protects the property of the pakehas. The Government fully recognise the merits and services of Poihipi and of the other loyal chiefs, and will assist them in making the roads, building the mills, and in the other good works which they contemplate. I am glad, also, to meet here to-day so many of the great tribe of the Ngatiraukawas. Matene Te Whiwhi, and many of that tribe, have welcomed me at Otaki, and now Hori Ngawhare is waiting to welcome me at Orakei-Korako. I rejoice that so many of the chiefs of the old times—the old trees of the forest—are still standing; and that a noble growth of young trees is rising around them. I trust that you will join with the Government in founding schools here, such as those already established at Pakowhai, Maketu, and elsewhere, in which the youth of the Maori race learn the language and arts of the English. As I said at Tokano the other day, there was once a time when the ancestors of the English were little more advanced in civilisation than the Maoris now are; but wise and good men arose among them, and taught them to make roads, and to build ships and houses. About the time that Hongi, the Ngapuhi chief, went to England, a Scotchman, McAdam, discovered how best to make roads, and his is the system now in use both in England and in New Zealand. You have not to make new discoveries for yourselves, but only to adopt the useful discoveries of your pakeha friends. What Poihipi said in his speech just now was correct. Each tribe can do what it likes within its own boundaries. For example: Whenever a tribe wishes to make roads, the Government will assist with money and tools; and no other tribe has any right to interfere. The Government has no desire to make roads, or other useful works, except in those districts where the Maoris willingly co-operate. You already understand the advantage of roads. A horse does not cost so much feed as a man, and yet it is eight times as strong. When you have got roads, one man with a horse and cart can carry as much corn or potatoes as eight men could carry. As there are no other points on which you wish to address me, I will now conclude. I thank you once more for the hearty welcome you have given me, and pray that peace and prosperity may flourish among you, like the everlasting green of your native forests.

At the conclusion of his Excellency's speech, which was received with cheers by the natives assembled, the natives danced hakas and other Maori dances.

Afterwards his Excellency visited the falls of the Waikato, situated amidst fine scenery, about four miles from the point at which the river issues from the northern end of the lake. There are fine rapids above and below the falls; which resemble in height and volume of water those of the Rhine at Schaffhausen. After visiting the falls the party bathed in one of the natural hot baths in the neighbourhood, where a cascade of tepid water falls into a rocky basin.

April 13.—The Governor and suite, leaving with regret the shores of the great lake, or sea ("moana," not "roto," as the natives call it) of Taupo, and, after four hours' easy riding over fern-clad hills for about 25 miles, reached Orakei-Korako, a native kainga on the left bank of the Waikato, belonging to the clan of the Ngatiraukawa. Here the Governor was welcomed by the influential chief Hori Ngawhare, who, though in extreme old age and infirmity, had travelled more than 50 miles to meet his Excellency. This portion of the Ngatiraukawa had been in former years engaged in the rebellion. Several chiefs, however, had gone to meet the Governor at Taupo, to invite him to their country; and he was received by the assembled clan with the most hearty respect. The substance of the speeches delivered at Orakei-Korako is as follows :—

HOHEPA TAUPIRI: Come, O Governor, come and see us, your people. You are the father of the people. (Song of welcome.) Salutations to you,

O Governor. We have been swimming, as it were, in the ocean, and knew not where to go. We feel that we are now touching the shore, and you have come to help and guide us to land. Salutations to you, O Governor.

Tuiri Rangihoro: Salutations, O Governor! Come and see us. We hand over all the roads in this district to you; they are in your hands. It is for you to direct what should be done here. Salutations!

Hare Matenga: Salutations! Come, O Governor, and visit us. We rejoice to see you here. We shall ever remain faithful to the Government. The people and the pas are all yours; we cann't say more.

Aranui: Welcome, O Govern'r! Come and clear away the doubts and darkness that surround us. Come and see Hori Ngawhare. We have long been searching for a proper course to take, so as to save the people. We are now beginning to think we have found out the right way. You have now arrived, and we will listen to you, in hope that our troubles may now end. All the Ngatiraukawa, and the followers of the King, will hear what you say to-day. Salutations to you.

Hori Ngawhare: Come, O Governor, and search for yourself what is required for us. We are searching, we, the Maoris, for a proper course. We wish you, O Governor, to point out to us what to do.

His Excellency Sir G. F. Bowen then addressed the meeting to the following effect :—O my friends, Hori Ngawhare and chiefs of Ngatiraukawa, salutations to you all. I thank you for your loyal speeches, and am very glad to visit you in your own country. I also rejoice to meet your celebrated chief Hori Ngawhare, and am sorry to find him suffering in body, though his mind is as clear as ever. I thank him for having travelled 50 miles to meet me here, and for his invitation to escort me through your country from Taupo to Cambridge, in the Waikato. I am glad that the Ngatiraukawas desire to see the Governor crossing their district. I know that there are two roads from here to Auckland, and that both are equally safe for me. Next time I will go by your road, but this time I will go by Rotorua and Tauranga, where I have promised to meet your friend, Mr. McLean, to consult with him how best to promote the interests of the Maoris. One of your chiefs (Tuiri) said, in his speech, that the Ngatiraukawas place the question of roads entirely in the hands of the Governor ; but, my friends, this is a question principally for yourselves. Each tribe should say whether it will assist the Government in making roads in its own district, and no other tribe has any right to interfere, as I have explained at Taupo and elsewhere. The benefits of roads are great, and affect the Maoris equally with the pakehas ; indeed, there are as yet but few pakehas in these inland districts. I am very glad to find that the Ngatiraukawas wish for roads, and the Government will assist you with money and tools, as it is assisting other tribes. Remember that roads do not affect the mana of the chiefs or the ownership of the land. This is quite clear. Let no man deceive you on this point. The telegraph is also of great use to the

Maoris. Formerly, if a Maori wanted a bag of flour from Napier or Tauranga he had to send a messenger for it, and to incur much delay and expense. Now, he can send for it by the wire, and it comes up by the coach at once. In addition to the roads and the telegraph, I recommend to you the foundation of schools for your children; the Government will assist you also in this matter. As there are no other points on which you wish me to address you, I will conclude by again thanking you for the hearty welcome which you have given me.

After the korero was over, his Excellency bathed in the warm baths on the bank of the Waikato river.

From this point two routes to Auckland were open to the Governor. He could proceed in two days' ride to Cambridge, in the Waikato delta, whence there is (as has already been said) a carriage road to Auckland, which city could be reached in this way in three or four days. The Ngatiraukawas urged his Excellency to adopt this route, which lies for the most part through their territory, and offered to escort him to Cambridge. But the Governor preferred the other and longer, though more interesting, road by the hot lakes and Tauranga, at which latter place he had, before leaving Napier, arranged to meet Mr. McLean, the Minister for Native Affairs; who, while the Governor was crossing the central districts, had been doing good service by visiting, in the Government steamer, the natives scattered along the East Coast of the island, especially those of the loyal clan of the Ngatiporou.

Accordingly, on the 14th, at 8 a.m., the Governor

crossed the Waikato in a canoe, and visited the magnificent alum cave on its right bank, together with the neighbouring geysers. At 9.30 a.m., the party started on horseback for Kaiteriria (25 miles), which was reached at 5 p.m., after a halt of two hours at a hot stream about halfway, where the entire party enjoyed a delicious swim in the tepid water.

Kaiteriria is a small pa on the picturesque lake Rotokakahi, and is one of the posts held by a detachment of the native Militia, commanded here by Captain Mair. The Arawas composing the force are fine young men, well drilled according to English discipline, who have done good service in the war against their rebel countrymen. Kaiteriria is a convenient head-quarters from which to visit Rotomahana (the hot lake *par excellence*) and other parts of the wondrous lake district, of which no description will be attempted here. The reader of these notes is referred to the books of Dr. Hochstetter and Lieutenant Meade, and to several papers in the Transactions of the New Zealand Institute. On the 15th the Governor started at 8.30 a.m., and in three hours rode over the hills by a rugged path of fourteen miles to Lake Rotomahana, while others of the party proceeded thither by a canoe across Lake Tarawera. As the Governor had on a previous occasion, eighteen months ago, stayed for two days at Rotomahana when accompanying thither H.R.H. the Duke of Edinburgh, he now remained there only a few hours, re-visiting the famous white and pink terraces, and then returned on horseback to Kaiteriria.

On the 16th the party started at 10 a.m., and, after a delightful ride of 12 miles along the shores of the beautiful lakes Rotokakahi and Tikitapu, and afterwards along the margin of Lake Rotorua, reached Ohinemutu, the principal inland settlement of the great clan of the Arawa. The afternoon was spent in swimming in the tepid waters of the Lake, and in visiting the geysers of this wonderful place, so renowned in Maori song and legend. A strong contrary wind rendered impossible a visit to the island of Mokoia, the scene of the story of Hine Moa, the Hero, and of her lover Tutanekai, the Leander, of Polynesian mythology. In the evening the Governor held a korero with several of the Arawa chiefs, who, like their countrymen elsewhere, were all eager for the extension of roads and schools.

Having visited on former occasions Maketu, the chief Arawa settlement on the sea coast, the Governor on the 17th determined to proceed from Ohinemutu to Tauranga by a new and direct road now nearly completed by native labour. It was a ride of 38 miles, of which 18 were through the forest, and the road reflects great credit on the officers in charge of this difficult work. We may take the opportunity of mentioning that, as we are informed, the Governor has expressed much satisfaction at the tact and ability displayed by the civil officers immediately charged with the management of native affairs, and of public works in the interior of New Zealand, and with the good discipline and soldierlike appearance of the officers and men of the colonial forces.

At Mangarewa, in the heart of the forest, the Governor found triumphal arches erected in his honour by the Maoris employed on the road, who received him with shouts and chants of welcome. The party engaged in blasting rocks saluted his approach by firing several charges, which echoed like cannon-shots through the grand primeval forest. One of the working parties was headed by Ngatote, a brother of Kereopa, who was executed in January last for murder and rebellion.

Five miles from Tauranga the Governor was met by the Volunteer Cavalry of that town and district, who escorted him past the famous Gate Pa to the wharf, where the "Luna" lay at anchor, and where he was received by Mr. McLean and a guard of honour of the Rifle Volunteers. It may be remarked that the Volunteers at Tauranga comprise one-fifth of the entire population of the district—men, women, and children. This is as if the Volunteers in the United Kingdom numbered six millions instead of two hundred thousand.

April 18.—The morning was spent in visiting the cemetery, where the officers and men of the Imperial forces killed at the Gate Pa in 1864 were interred, and in transacting business with several Maori chiefs. The Ngaiterangis, who fought so bravely against the English in the late war, are now the firm friends and allies of the Government. Two of their chiefs volunteered to escort the Governor overland to Ohinemuri by the difficult Katikati pass, so long closed to Europeans. Accordingly the "Luna," leaving Tauranga at 2 p.m., landed the Governor and his native guides at 4.30 p.m. at Katikati, where they passed the night in a small house belonging to Mr. Faulkner.

On the following morning, the 19th, the party started on horseback amid a deluge of rain, which lasted the whole day. This was the first bad weather which the Governor had met with throughout the whole journey from Napier. The streams and rivers to be forded were very much swollen, and the path through the forest, in the latter part of the ride of 28 miles, was positively dangerous. However, the Governor reached Ohinemuri safely before dark, and on the next morning, the 20th, was received by Mr. McLean on board the "Luna," which had come round Cape Colville and up the river Thames. A large meeting of natives was being held at Ohinemuri, for a "tangi" on account of the death of the cele-brated chief Taraia. Several leading chiefs from various parts of the island had accompanied Mr. McLean in the "Luna," and now joined in the "tangi." When it was over, a "korero" was held, at which the Governor and the Minister for Native Affairs addressed the assembled tribes. We annex the substance of the speeches delivered.

WIKIRIWHI rose and welcomed the visitors as follows: Welcome, Governor, welcome, Mr. McLean, to the place of Taraia's death. Come and see the death of Taraia, and express your regret to the people who last saw him. His soul has gone, taken hence by the strong hand of Death. Welcome, O people. Welcome, Ngatiraukawa and Ngatikahungunu. Come and express your sorrow at the departure of the Taraia of New Zealand; himself selected the day for his departure. Welcome, Ngaiterangi. Had he been bound with chains it had not been possible to detain him. Though his spirit has fled, his voice still lives, and bids you all welcome.

MOWATI KIHAROA: Farewell. The forms of death are varied. Some fall from trees, and die; others die in their houses; others again fall in battle; but these are all ways in which chiefs may die. It is a broad and open road, and you can see them go and sorrow at their departure. We come hither to show our affection. The men of great name whom you knew, Taraia, have gone. You have gone to them, and now farewell. Other people of yours have disappeared whose canoes you commanded.

[Song] Farewell, farewell! I greet you, the people who last saw his face.

ROPATA TE ABAKAI: Welcome, Governor and Mr. McLean. Come and see the death—the death of Taraia. It is right to show grief on this occasion, to come to the death of Taraia. What can we do? Who can avoid the stroke of death? Welcome, people who have come in accordance with the usages of our ancestors. Welcome to Hauraki. Bring hither those griefs and lay them in the spot where Taraia died. Nothing can be done now beyond bidding you welcome.

TAREHA: Bid us welcome. Welcome your friends the Governor and Mr. McLean, and bid us welcome also according to our usual custom. The voices now are not like the old voices; it is a different voice now. We come, we come, to see the death of Taraia. The grief now displayed by the Governor is not only now shown for the first time—it has been already seen at the other deaths which have occurred in this land. Taraia is dead, and here is the Governor come to mingle his tears with yours, and to mourn with Te Hira. Welcome your friend the Governor and your man, Mr. McLean. These are the chiefs showing love to the people of the land. Your old chief as well as ours has gone, but here is your old friend come to see you. Wherever grief is felt there are the Governor and Mr. McLean to alleviate the distress. When troubles arise there they are to put them down and restore order and tranquillity. There is now only one thing wanting: that is, a Maori chief to accompany the Governor and your friend Mr. McLean wherever they go. [Song.]

APANUI : Why is it you mention Ngatiraukawa, as if that were the only tribe connected with Taraia ? Bid us welcome. Here we come. We are all related to Taraia. Why do not you mention Ngaiterangi, Ngatiawa, Ngatikahungunu, and other tribes, all of whom are also related to Taraia ? We have come to the spot where Taraia's body lay. When the sun comes near to setting, he sinks rapidly. What can we do ? The road is broad and open ; it has been travelled by our ancestors from olden times. [Song] Farewell, farewell, my father.

MOANANUI : Welcome, welcome, people of the land. Welcome. There are few to welcome you.

Come to Hauraki. Welcome to Jordan; leave Egypt
behind you. Come to Jordan, my friends. Welcome
each and all of you. Welcome, you my friends who
nave come to the death of Taraia, come in order that
we may speak mouth-to-mouth at Jordan. Because
of others not holding similar views to those which we
hold, they fled away. However you will not be able
to reply to my remarks. I shall touch to-day upon all
those matters. I do not go to this place and that
place to collect my knowledge, but you will not be
able to reply to me. Welcome, my friends—come as
you have come, well disposed, to see my face; do not
think I am not glad to see you. Come and see your
brother Taraia. Whatever precautions people may
take they cannot avert death. Come to see the
foolishness of Hauraki; there is no knowledge in
Hauraki, come and see it. Welcome, my father, bring
the people of the land to see us; they would not have
come had it not been for you. Welcome, my father:
bring hither your guests to see the foolishness of the
people of this place. Come hither, my father, from
the place where you have been laying down life-giving
principles of action.

Mr. McLean made a few remarks, which were
listened to attentively by the natives. We understood
him to refer to the visit of the Governor and the
several chiefs who accompanied him from different
parts of the island. In reference to Taraia he said
that he had departed in the usual course from old age
on the road from which no traveller ever returns. The
Hauhau prophets said that their dead would come to

life to re-people the island; if they were able to bring
Taraia to life again he would believe them, but, if not,
they must see it was full time to cast off their silly
delusions.   In no instance had they seen people who
had trodden the paths of death return again to re-
people the earth.   Idle rumours were in circulation
that an attack was to be made on the Ohinemuri
natives by Major Ropata of Ngatiporou.   Such a
report was without any foundation.   The present visit
was merely paid to exchange friendly sentiments;
and, as the Governor was so seldom a visitor to
Ohinemuri, he expected to hear Te Hira, who was
present, give expression to his views and feelings.

The GOVERNOR then spoke to the following
effect :—Salutations to you, my friends.   I thank you
for the welcome you have given me.   This is my
second visit to Ohinemuri, and I have received a
hearty welcome on each occasion.   My first visit was
made four years ago; and your celebrated chief
Taraia then welcomed me in person.   He was a great
chief in war, and a great friend to the pakeha in peace.
He was known to all the tribes throughout the island
as the principal chief of Hauraki.   I heard with great
pain of his death, and am now come to join you in
lamenting him.   I have arrived, accompanied by chiefs
from different parts of the island, who, like me, have
heard of his death and regret it.   I have now been
through all the native districts from Wellington
northwards.   I have seen the Ngatikahungunu at
Napier, the Ngatituwharetoa at Taupo, the Ngatirau-

kawa at Orakei-Korako, the Arawa at Ohinemutu, the Ngaiterangi at Tauranga; and I have now come here among you, the Ngatimaru and Ngatitamatera. Everywhere I have found the death of Taraia regretted. However, if the old chiefs, the aged trees of the forest, are falling, I am glad to see such a fine growth of young men to take their place. I have not much to say to you on this occasion, except to thank you for the welcome you have given me, to tell you I shall be glad to come again to see you, and to wish you all happiness and prosperity.

Te Hira: Welcome, Governor. All I can do is to greet you. I cannot make myself one with you so thoroughly as your friends around you have because our thoughts are not yet the same; but when I find that I can dwell quietly and without being disturbed on my own place, then, perhaps, I shall see my way clear to do as the others have done. Although your friend Taraia is dead, he is but one man. It were better that the position of the land were made clear. My hands are quite clean. As soon as I hear your word that my land shall be mine, then I shall be clear. Welcome, O people. I do not know your thoughts. There is no course of action decided upon here. Come when you like. Unite yourselves to us now to-day, because it has been through you that this place is what it is.

It will be remembered that Ohinemuri has long been one of the principal strongholds of Hauhauism and rebellion. Yet it will be seen that the Governor was

heartily welcomed by all parties. It may be mentioned
that in honour of his arrival, Union Jacks were hoisted
in every place where formerly floated Hauhau flags.

April 21.—This day being Sunday, the "Luna"
remained quietly at anchor at Ohinemuri, and was
visited by large numbers of the natives.

On the 22nd, at 8 a.m., the Governor and
Mr. McLean proceeded up the river Thames (so
Captain Cook named the noble river called Waiho by
the Maoris) for about fifteen miles above the junction
of the Ohinemuri Creek; that is, to a point about
forty miles from the mouth of the river. For several
miles above Ohinemuri the river runs through the
forest; further on the open country begins. The
Governor and party here ascended the hill " Te Rae o
te Papa," that is, the brow of the plain, whence there
is one of the most extensive and interesting prospects
in all New Zealand. Below, the eye ranges over the
whole of the wide valley or plain watered by the rivers
Thames and Piako, with their numerous tributaries,
from the sea to the north as far as the mountains
round Lake Taupo to the south. On a clear day
Tongariro and the snowy ridge of Ruapehu are clearly
visible, as well as Tauhara, the remarkable mountain
at the north end of Lake Taupo. To the east is the
richly-wooded Aroha mountain, in which the gold-
bearing cordillera of the Cape Colville peninsula
appears to terminate. To the west are the bush-
covered ranges hanging over the Piako river, and
where these end there is an extensive prospect over
the plains of the Waikato, bounded by the Pirongia

mountain, which is not far distant from the West Coast of the North Island.

The great plain of the Thames is still almost without cultivation or human habitation, with the exception of a few Maori villages; yet, in all human probability, the time is not far distant when it will be covered with flourishing English farms and heids of cattle and sheep. The Thames already supplies a liquid highway, and the goldfields near its mouth a ready market for pastoral and agricultural produce.

On his return to Ohinemuri the Governor was present at the arrival of a large number of visitors from various tribes, who had come, according to Maori custom, to join in the lament ("tangi") for Taraia—a ceremony resembling the coronach of the old Scottish Highlanders, and the "keen" of the Irish peasantry. The wailing of the women, and the chants celebrating the deeds of the departed chief, were very striking. It is considered a fortunate thing that the Governor visited Ohinemuri at a time when so many of the leading chiefs of the principal Maori clans were there assembled, and thus had an opportunity of paying their homage to the head of the Government.

April 23.—The "Luna," the largest vessel which had ever previously ascended the Thames, left Ohinemuri at 7 a.m. with the ebbing tide. Owing to the hitherto imperfect survey of the river, she grounded about two miles from the mouth, but floated again with the rising flood, and reached the wharf at Grahamstown at 5 p.m. On the 24th a deluge of rain having set in, the Governor was unable to visit the gold mines, but held a reception, at which were present the principal officers connected with the Thames and the leading residents. At 5 p.m. the "Luna" left Grahamstown, and, after landing some native chiefs at Taupo, arrived at Auckland at 11 o'clock p.m.

So ended an important and memorable journey.

APPENDIX.

It has been considered desirable to supplement the above interesting narrative with translations of several letters from Maori chiefs to the Agent-General, received by the last mail from New Zealand. These letters are not only remarkable for their poetic sentiment, but, coming as they do from leading men, they are a very significant index to the present state of the native mind.

Dr. Featherston, during a residence in the country of about thirty years, and during eighteen years' continuous tenure of office as Superintendent, was in constant official communication with the native tribes of the Wellington Province; and it is well known that during the disturbed period, from 1861 to 1865, the maintenance of peace in this portion of the Colony was in a great measure due to his personal influence with the Ngatiawa and Ngatiraukawa chiefs. It is satisfactory, therefore, to find that he is still remembered among them as their "friend and father," and that they continue to look to him for guidance and advice.

Wi Tako, the writer of the first letter, is a man of good birth and of considerable political influence. He was one of the chief promoters of the Maori-king Movement, and has always taken an active part in native affairs. In 1862 he withdrew himself from all communication with Europeans, fortified his pah at Waikanae, raised the rebel flag, and moved from place to place attended by a body guard of 100 armed men in uniform. At this time Sir George Grey, who had re-assumed the government of the Colony, visited the west coast settlements, and invited Wi Tako to meet him at Otaki. The rebel chief at first refused to receive the Governor except in his own pah and under the " King's " flag ; but through the personal influence of Dr. Featherston, he was ultimately induced to come out and meet his Excellency on neutral ground. Wi Tako afterwards took the oath of allegiance, and is now a valuable Government ally; but for a considerable time both he and his tribe were on the verge of open rebellion. In the Wellington Council Chamber there is a fine painting—paid for by public subscription—representing Dr. Featherston, as Superintendent of the Province, with Wi Tako and the veteran chief Epuni at his side, a picture full of historic interest to those who remember the early struggles of this part of the Colony.

IHAIA PORUTU is a young chief of a highly intelligent type, who lives in European fashion and conducts a small farm of his own in the valley of the Hutt. He is the son of Te Rira Porutu, who was a staunch friend of the Colonists in the early days of the Wellington Settlement. He is a native magistrate, and one of the assessors of the Native Lands Court.

WI PARATA and WI TAMIHANA are chiefs of the Ngatiawa tribe, the former being now one of the Maori representatives in the General Assembly.

The writers of the other letters are representative chiefs of the warlike clans of Wanganui. Aperaniko's letter recalls the tragic events of Moutoa. In the year 1863, a band of Hauhau fanatics were making a descent on the town of Wanganui, but were met and repulsed by a body of friendly natives from the lower Wanganui district. The main fight took place on the island of Moutoa, about fifty miles up the river, and a number of Maoris were killed on both sides. Dr. Featherston, as General Government Agent, was immediately on the spot and took steps to prevent a recurrence of hostilities. He armed the friendlies, fortified the river against further attack, established confidence among the settlers, and caused a handsome marble monument to be erected in the town of Wanganui to the memory of the brave men who fell at Moutoa. But, as will presently appear, Dr. Featherston has other claims to what one of his correspondents terms the "fidelity of the tribes to their absent chief." Major Kepa and Captain Aperaniko served with the Native Contingent under Major-General Chute in his celebrated Taranaki campaign; and the former of these chiefs received, as the gift of the Queen, a handsome sword, in recognition of his loyalty and valorous conduct in the field. This native force, composed of the best men of the Lower Wanganui, Ngatiapa and Rangitane tribes, was organised and commanded by Major (now Lt.-Col.) McDonnell; but this gallant officer was wounded at the commencement of the campaign, and the responsibility and control of the native allies then devolved on Dr. Featherston, who had accompanied the expedition as a Volunteer. The pen of the late Von Tempskey has described in graphic terms how Dr. Featherston kept the rival factions together and led them into action—

how he exposed his life on every occasion and stirred the natives to enthusiasm by his presence—how one pah after another fell before their assault, and how finally, in spite of the mutinous spirit of the younger chiefs, he succeeded in taking the Native Contingent through the memorable bush march at the rear of Mount Egmont.

It may readily be understood that such an example was not without its effect upon a people who almost adore personal courage, and that the expressions of devotion to their " fighting superintendent" are perfectly genuine and sincere. The benefit to the Colony of the personal services briefly alluded to above, may be inferred from the following passage in one of the published despatches *(Feb.* 12*th*, 1866*)* of Major-General Sir Trevor Chute, K.C.B.:—

"It is hardly possible for me to convey to your Excellency how much I feel indebted to Dr. Featherston, Superintendent of this Province, for his able advice on all subjects connected with the Maoris. He accompanied me throughout the campaign, sharing all our dangers and privations, and was present at each engagement and assault. I am particularly obliged to him for the zeal with which he has at all times laboured to obtain information of the movements and positions of the rebels, which it would have been almost impossible for me to acquire without his assistance."

1. LETTER FROM WI TAKO NGATATA.
(Translation.)

TE ARO PA,

WELLINGTON, *June 3rd*, 1872.

To DR. FEATHERSTON.

O father! Salutations! Long may you live! May

your life be spared beyond the usual term granted to man on earth! May God preserve you and your children!

O my loving friend Featherston, here is your letter of the 28th of March, which has reached me. Great has been our emotion over your letter, full of kind words to us and sentiments of regard for your Maori people. We respond to your kind words thus expressed, and we think mournfully of the wide sea that now divides us. Many days and many nights must pass before our bodies could reach each other, and our lips speak face to face. But the heart can travel across at once and hold communion with yours.

We shall never forget each other. Our regard for each other will never grow cold.

O father, I have nothing to tell you. There is only one thing to say: the island is at rest. Men of bad hearts may cause disturbance again, but now all is at peace. All I have to say is, salutations to you and your family!

There is nothing in my letter, but yours was full; the return I make is a poor one. But when you receive my letter you must send us another, and continue your good advice to us.

Again, here is another word. I have told you that the island is at peace. This is the result of the good policy of the present Government. They are securing the confidence of the people throughout the island. Ended.

I bid you farewell, O my father! Abide you and your family in your new home. Farewell!

From your friend of long standing,

WI TAKO NGATATA,

And from all the Ngatiawa tribe.

Father, you are remembered by all the tribes with affection. But, O father, many of the people that belonged to your tribes, the Ngatiawa and Ngatiraukawa are dead, having been carried off by fever.

Ended!

2. Letter from Ihaia Porutu.
(Translation.)

WELLINGTON,

June 8th, 1872.

To Dr. FEATHERSTON.

Friend, salutations! Your letters of the 28th of March, have arrived. I mean your letters to the native people of this Island. Friend, I send greeting to you, to your family, and to all your nation. Our love for you personally is very great. We have not forgotten all the good maxims you taught us, and the measures you proposed for our benefit. You are in a far-off land now, but the hearts of men can follow you, and day and night we remember your goodness. This is only a letter of remembrance from me.

Your loving friend,

IHAIA PORUTU.

(*Native Magistrate.*)

---

3. Letter from Aperaniko Taiawhio.
(Translation.)

WANGANUI TOWN,

May 30th, 1872.

To Dr. FEATHERSTON.

Friend, salutations! I have received your letter. Great was my delight to find that your affection was strong enough to make its way across the wide sea and reach us here.

We are separated—you far off in one direction and we far off in the other—but our regard for each other is as lasting and enduring as ever!

Enough on that subject; here is another matter. On the 17th of this month there was a meeting at Putiki (a great and important meeting), and Metekingi was the host. The object of the meeting was to give a welcome to Pehi Turoa and Topine,*

---

* Late leaders of the rebel party.

on the occasion of their visit to Putiki. The meeting assembled
in the house known as "Matapihi." On this occasion the name
was changed to "Aomarama" (*lit.* the intelligent world as
distinguished from the benighted). The house of Pelhi and
Topine at Ohinemutu was "Te Aomarama," and the symbol is
intended to embrace all New Zealand. Waikato came, a hundred
strong, with Rewi* at their head. Nothing but words of peace
and goodwill were heard within the walls of Te Aomarama.

Afterwards Topine returned our hospitalities. The house
was called "Hikurangi," and the meeting took place at
Taumarunui.

I went—so did Mete and Haimona and Pehi and Topia and
Te Tahana, in response to the invitation. Mete applied for the
child of Uenukutuwhatu. Topine gave the woman (in marriage).
The object of this gift was to cement this good understanding,
and secure a pledge of future peace between the Pakehas and
Maoris. The talk ended at Te Matapihi. The tribes who
assembled there were Ngatiraukawa, Ngatikahungunu, and
Waikato. Tahana Turoa spoke thus: "Listen, ye tribes
assembled in this house! Mete now has the child of Uenukutuwhatu, to be nursed by Wanganui. I call on all the tribes to
bear witness." Then rose Pehi Turoa: "I agree," said he, "that
there shall be peace on this river—from the mouth thereof even
to the source."

Hip! Hip! Hurrah!! shouted the whole assembly present
at this meeting.

Pehi has arrived and is living in the town. This is all the
news from this place. Mr. Richard Woon, the native resident
magistrate, took part in these proceedings.

Ended.

From your loving Son,
APERANIKO TAIAWHIO,
(Captain of Native Forces and Chief of
Lower Wanganui.)

---

* The fighting general of the Waikato.

4. LETTER FROM WI PARATA, M.H.R.

(*Translation.*)

WAIKANAE,
NEW ZEALAND
May 26*th*, 1872.

To DR. FEATHERSTON.

Friend and father, salutations! Great is my affection
for you. Although your body is so far away, when your letters
reached us and we read them it was just as if you were present.

Although the ocean is so broad, the affection of the heart and
all affairs of importance will still go over to you.

I have received the letter which you addressed to us on the
28th March.

Friend, great was our rejoicing when we saw your letter
and read your words of greeting to the tribes whom you had left
behind. The fidelity of your native tribes to their absent chief
has not diminished.

Friend, good indeed are your words of congratulation about
the restoration of peace in this island.

Friend, during the month of March that is past I travelled
through the disturbed districts of Ngatiruanui and Taranaki, and
I saw all the people, both good and bad. I had interviews with
all the chiefs of these tribes. I saw Titoko-Waru and Wiremu
Kingi and Te Whiti also, and they all talked with me. The
burden of all their speeches was this, that they would give up
fighting and bring all their grievances to the General Assembly.

Wiremu Kingi also said that he would leave Waitara* in my
hands to be dealt with by the Assembly.

I tell you this in order that you may know the mind of your
former friends who have now returned to their allegiance. If
the lands† which have thus been placed in my hands to be dealt
with by the Assembly should be always held back, then your
good wishes for this island will be void.

Friend, it is right that you should bring this desire of the
Taranaki, Ngatiruanui and Ngatiawa tribes before the Parliament

---

* The land dispute which occasioned the Taranaki War.
† Refers to the confiscated lands.

of England, because you have been appointed by our Queen to bear the burdens of this island into her presence. For this reason am I telling you of the burdens laid before me by the tribes who have been punished.

Friend, these are the most important questions with the tribes of this island—these relating to their lands. I have therefore thought that it will be for you in England to set the minds of the New Zealand people at rest on these questions. Ended.

From your loving Son,

WI PARATA, M. H. R.

LETTER FROM WI TAMIHANA.
(*Translation.*)
WELLINGTON,
July 1st, 1872.

TO DR. FEATHERSTON.

Salutations to you and to your children! Salutations also to the great men of the nation among whom you are now living.

Friend, your letter of the 28th March, 1872, has reached me. I read it aloud in the hearing of the elders of the Ngatitoa and Ngatiawa tribes. All present at the meeting, men and women, old and young, joined their voices in a "mihi" (lament) for you as they thought of your face, and then of the broad sea intervening.

Father, here am I still bearing you in remembrance, and your name is of frequent mention among us. Friend, great is my sorrow on account of the ravages of the present fever. Here are three men lying dead! All the chiefs of Ngatiawa, Ngatitoa, and Ngatiraukawa are dying off, and my grief on this account is great.

Friend, I have nothing to write about from this place—simply to express our great love for you.

I send greeting to you, and to your family, and to all your people.

Ended.

From your attached Friend,
WIREMU TAMIHANA TE NEKE,
(Christian Teacher and Native
Magistrate.)

LETTER FROM MAJOR KEEPA.
(Translation.)
PUTIKI PA,
WANGANUI,
July 3rd, 1872.

To DR. FEATHERSTON.

O sire, salutations! I send greeting to the greatest of our benefactors—to one whose love has been felt by those who are dead and gone, as well as by the living!

O sire, salutations! Your letter has been received, and both I and my tribe have seen it. Great is my satisfaction that you should still remember us, residing, as you now are, in the midst of the great world, and near the fountain of life!

O sire, the reports of what you are doing have reached this country. We are greatly rejoiced, because all your plans are clear and comprehensive. Was it not through the clearness of your plans that our troubles in this land were brought to an end ? Did you not encourage and direct us, your Maori children, in the days of fighting, and help us to put down the evil? Was it not through your work that peace was finally established among us?

O sire, continue to exert your influence on behalf of the Maori tribes. You know me, and you know my works. You know that I and my tribe strove to maintain the Queen's

E

authority in this land, when all was dark and threatening. You know it all.

I shall continue to write to you often in the days that are coming.

Long may you live, and may peace be with you!

From your loving friend,

MEIHA KĘPA TE RANGIHIWINUI,

(*Head Chief of the Lower Wanganui tribes, and Major of Native Militia.*)

LETTER FROM METEKINGI PAETAHI.

PUTIKI,
July, 3*rd*, 1872.

TO DR. FEATHERSTON.

O, our loving father! Salutations to you yonder, seeking out the advantage of this country. We have received your letters, and greatly pleased were we with your words.

You saved this island in its time of trouble. When you left, peace had prevailed.

Friend Featherston, salutations! Here am I still doing my good work. I am constantly calling to the "Hauhaus" to come in and unite with us in devising some good measures for New Zealand.

Friend Featherston, salutations again! Often I remember all your good counsels, and all your friendly acts; how you came to Wanganui, when all was dark and evil, and continued your work till all was quiet, and then went away to England. Although that country is distant enough, the affection of the heart appears to bring it near.

O sire Featherston, place this letter of mine before the Government of England, in order that they may see how the country has been quieted under your management.

You have, perhaps, heard of my great meeting, known as
"Te Matapihi," when all the tribes assembled at Putiki.

This is all I have to say to you. My words are few, but they
are, nevertheless, full of love and affection for you.

From your true friend,
METEKINGI PAETAHI,
(*Formerly Maori representative in the
General Assembly.*)